B   400

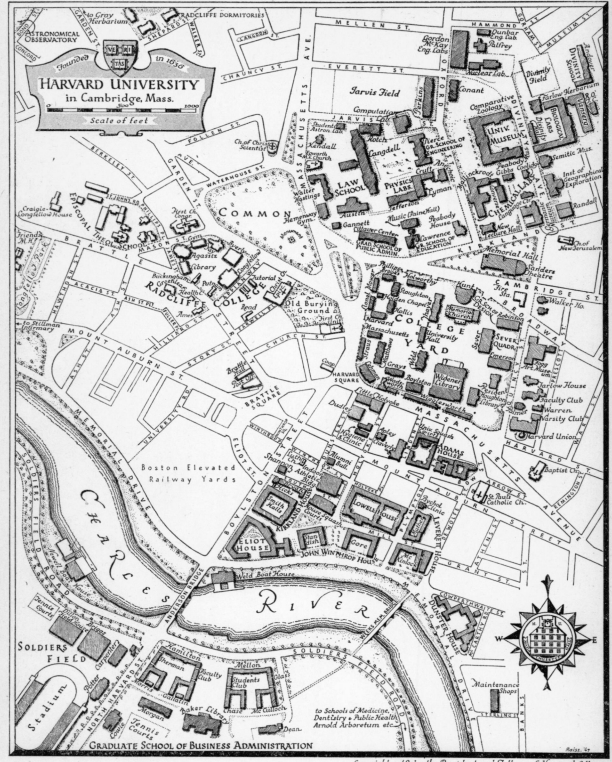

VERITAS

Founded in 1636

HARVARD UNIVERSITY
in Cambridge, Mass.

0 500 1000
Scale of feet

GRADUATE SCHOOL OF BUSINESS ADMINISTRATION

Raisz '47

FAIR HARVARD

The Class of 1876 Gate to the Yard between Stoughton and Holworthy.

Fair Harvard

PHOTOGRAPHS BY

SAMUEL CHAMBERLAIN

WITH TEXT BY DONALD MOFFAT

HARVARD UNIVERSITY PRESS · CAMBRIDGE · 1948

ACKNOWLEDGMENTS

Grateful acknowledgment is made to W. G. Land, '28, compiler of the *Harvard University Handbook*, for the factual data used in the legends for this book; and in particular to Samuel Eliot Morison, '07, for the predatory use made of his admirable *Three Centuries of Harvard* in both legends and introduction. The debt owed Professor Morison by every writer on Harvard, and indeed by every Harvard man, is immeasurable. Thanks are also due to the Ware Collection of Blaschka Glass Models of Plants for a photograph, and to the Cruft Laboratory for the view of the Anechoic Chamber.

CONTENTS

CONTENTS—*Continued*

ONE VIEW OF HARVARD

HERE and there in the pages of Samuel Eliot Morison's *Three Centuries of Harvard* occurs a phrase which might well have been taken for the College motto, to stand beside the celebrated *Veritas*: "Harvard men were divided in opinion."

In a present alumni army of some ninety thousand you will find, where Harvard is concerned, no two elements agreeing on anything. Among undergraduates the same law runs, and among the faculty too. Harvard means conflict and conflict means passion and the only sensible rule for identifying a Harvard man is to call him a minority of one. United by a mystic loyalty which not only cements the family but forms a useful shield to hold up against the world, Harvard is rent by polite but fearful discord on every point worth mentioning from the function of education to the function of the catch in rowing. There is no escaping this truth, which is called John's Law, after the founder. Historians are sharply divided on the question of John Harvard's right to the title of founder.

For if education may be defined in a word, that word is controversy. Where concord reigns, learning withers; where conflict rules, it flourishes. And the cumulative effect of three hundred years of conflict results—in the best, or Harvard, opinion—in a university three times as great as one which has been at it only one hundred years, and so on.

Harvard can point to no moment in her history and truthfully say, "Here we were in equilibrium." No college generation has known an armistice in the age-old war between the orthodox and the radical, the conservative and the progressive points of view towards current controversy among her student or faculty scholar-servants, whether it be academic, religious, political, social, or trivial. Every day is crisis day at Harvard, and on few of them, be it said to her credit, has she failed to take the line leading up and on.

She has been called godless from the beginning, a serious charge during her first two hundred years, when religious orthodoxy was the only passport to fair repute; and radical almost as long as godless. In fact, the dangerous radical at godless Harvard emerges as a stock figure in her history. Yet the important point is this: in all the long roster of Harvard heretics and rebels I find no instance of a student or teacher being disciplined purely because of his opinions. In this respect Harvard's tradition stands firm as a rock, the record is clear. Tomorrow's dissenters like yesterday's may be reviled by the press, the public, and the pulpit; they may be, as they have been, called atheist, imperialist, communist, or merely un-American: the College fathers will uphold their right to be heard. Of this we may be sure.

Proof that Harvard has been well and wisely led over the long years — even if wisdom has often to be that of the serpent — may be found in the fact that almost every academic innovation has first been stigmatized as the last nail in old Harvard's coffin, then gradually accepted as part of the traditional pattern. ("Is it possible?" cried Mr. George, in a tone of great astonishment. "What?" asked Rollo, "Why, to find the inscription which was wickedly placed upon University Hall is not effaced, though years have elapsed." Rollo looked and saw in faint black capitals the following inscription: "The University is going to Hell!")* The point is that the progressive idea has always won out in the end, and its sponsor has always had the right to be heard. However, as Morison truly says, the opposition has seldom failed to make itself felt: "Important elements of New England society . . . looked with extreme disfavor on educational institutions which sought to prepare their alumni for the age in which they were to live, and sought to advance knowledge rather than to embalm it."

While a generation of man is put at thirty-three years, a college generation is only an eighth as long. In a sense, therefore, Harvard has survived not merely ten ages but something nearer seventy-five, a fact which makes it even more surprising that she has been able to cling so firmly to her greatest tradition, that of academic freedom, nourished by the doctrine of individual liberty. The story of human society testifies to the fact that freedom has been gained, an inch at a time, only by fighting. The right to it can never be assumed. Though freedom is a natural instinct, it is not a natural growth: eternally it has to be won again. And it is good that the universities should be, as they have always been, freedom's womb and greatest nursery, for the primary function of all education is to teach man how to be free.

Harvard's own history proves, even by the most grudging estimate, that she has not only held her gains in the everlasting struggle, but that her sons have always been among the leaders in the wider field of social progress. Whether it is cause or effect— whether Harvard stands on the side of liberalism because that is her tradition, or whether her tradition is the metal which attracts free minds to her service— is hard to say. Probably both premises support the conclusion. Of all her traditions, however, her concern for freedom, mother of controversy, is the dominant one.

Such a tradition has its drawbacks. At Harvard it has laid her open to certain accusations which on the whole are well founded. Allegations of Harvard snobbishness, Harvard heresy, and Harvard independence are among the inevitable defects of her preoccupation with freedom. Seventy-odd generations of Harvard students and teachers have refused to be regimented, to be told what to think and say, what to do, how to talk, how to dress, how to behave. The College authorities, uneasily aware of her reputation, have tried from time to time the experiment of "making Harvard more democratic." The fact that students were ranked according to their families' social standing in the community till 1769, when alphabetic ranking was introduced, is evidence that democratic equality had been a pesky problem long before that time. Compulsory Commons, the Harvard Union the House Plan, and many another scheme has been dedicated to the proposition that if students are thrown together they must automatically contract "democracy," like measles. And still in their off hours the ornery critters blandly continue on the obvious path of hobnobbing together on the basis of common tastes, manners, interests, accents, backgrounds, of "speaking the same language." It sounds suspiciously like human nature at work, and may indeed be just that.

And yet—though Harvard subscribes readily to the definition of democracy as a leveling up, not down— the criticism is fairly based. Time may or may not "make Harvard more democratic." The authorities wisely refrain from raising the issue, lest it turn and rend not only them, but the student and alumni bodies as well. Said gentle President Sparks at an 1850 faculty meeting when College discipline was under discussion, "Oh gentlemen, let the boys alone!"

Harvard is a benevolent autocracy operating under a tradition of change, fluidity, growth. A fast-running river is perhaps a good analogy—a white-water like any other New England stream, racing along over submerged rocks and hidden snags, leaping in falls, even occasionally resting in a quiet pool or meadow reach. But make no mistake: placid though it may appear on the surface, it is seething beneath. The American public, especially the non-New England public, have been generally deceived into ridiculing

---

*John T. Wheelright and Frederic J. Stimson, *Rollo's Journey to Cambridge.* Harvard Lampoon, 1879.

Harvard as a stagnant backwater of conventionality, the funeral home of conservatism. In this they are mistaken. They have been fooled by a natural tendency to confuse Harvard with Boston, just as they confound the Boston accent, from which the letter *r* is eliminated, with that of the University. The Boston influence is strong, to be sure, especially in Harvard's governing boards. But the long view must convince the most skeptical that this conservatism has had a beneficial effect on Harvard's steady growth. The undergraduate comes to Cambridge, stays four years or longer, and goes. Proper Boston— solid, incorruptible, immovable, but as devoted to the rights of the individual as Harvard herself— Boston stays; and provides, by no means incidentally, the pool of shrewdness and character from which the governing boards of Harvard have been largely drawn. Harvard's growth from a small theological school for the sons of gentlemen to a great university may rightly be attributed to the men of vision and genius who have served her well at critical moments in her history: a Dunster, a Leverett, an Eliot, a Conant, to cite only a few of her distinguished Presidents, not to mention the great scholars who in her service have advanced human knowledge. But the Overseers and the Fellows have played their inconspicuous part with practical common sense. They represent continuity.

Though their steadying influence may often have been exasperating, it has undoubtedly been beneficial. It would be amusing to compile a list of the many queer schemes, reforms, and innovations dreamed up on occasion by the undergraduates alone—impatient of tradition, quick against injustice, longing for immediate action. Student rebellions seem almost to have been the rule rather than the exception in Harvard history. The students have won many a good fight; but if all their enthusiastic proposals had been adopted the results would have been something less than useful. (A Student Council of President Lowell's regime suggested that "going out for something" be counted a half-course!)

The successful rebellions have been healthily numerous and prove, among other points, that modern high school "strikes" are no novelty. In the winter of 1675 the entire student body deserted Cambridge to affirm the unpopularity of President Hoar. One hundred years later President Holyoke said on his deathbed, after thirty-two years of office, "If any man wishes to be humbled and mortified, let him become President of Harvard College." In 1780, President Langdon was forced to resign in part as a result of a student memorial addressed to him in these words: "As a man of genius and knowledge we respect you; as a man of piety and virtue we venerate you; as a President we despise you." There were "bread-and-butter" rebellions as early as 1639, followed by others worthy of notice by College historians in 1766, 1805, and 1823 (the Great Rebellion against disciplinary measures when forty-three boys out of a class of seventy-five were expelled). Another took place in 1834 during the presidency of the unpopular Quincy, who dealt with a Yard riot by trying to dismiss the entire sophomore class, then committed the academic crime of invoking the Grand Jury of Middlesex County to proceed against individual offenders. "This," says Morison, "violated one of the oldest Harvard traditions: that the public authorities have no concern with what goes on inside a university, so long as the rights of outsiders are not infringed." Ever since then Harvard has looked after her own dirty linen with a fair regard for justice and expediency. Except in cases when the citizen is a sufferer, or when publicity detrimental to the University's reputation has been too flagrant to overlook, official policy has wisely followed the advice of President Sparks and, so far as possible, "let the boys alone." Though better bread-and-butter may often have been the object of undergraduate intransigence, the cause has usually been a question of individual liberty. And this is as it should be.

The Alumni Bulletin prints many of the letters it receives from Harvard graduates, letters characterized by their passion rather than their numbers. And though I am told by the editor that while two camps may quickly form on a moot point like, say, the site of a new library, a teachers' oath bill, or the form of a war memorial, within each camp the warriors glare and jostle, apparently quite unaware that the question of teachers' oaths (the word is used in its legal sense) had arisen in 1699, 1747, and 1783 with respect to religious orthodoxy, and in 1935 to political; or that a dispute about the form of a memorial to Harvard's dead likewise is hardly a novelty in her history. So the battle is set anew, with the functionalists drawn up across the valley from the non-funcs, watching like cats each others' campfires twinkling in the dark. Then, just as one side is ready to prime their pieces and charge, it appears that no two warriors can agree on tactics. Shall it be a bell tower, a students' activities center, a scholarship plan, a fish-hatchery in the Stadium?

Across the way the enemy argues the pros and cons of a simple granite shaft and an arch of triumph.

Committees are appointed, the question is debated in word and print, a decision is reached, money is raised, the plan is carried out, the democratic method is vindicated again, and everyone, winner and loser alike, is immensely displeased.

Thus Harvard has grown—rather like the British Constitution in some respects, in which tradition and the written word have equal force. But her traditions, unlike her years, are young and supple. Harvard was founded only a century and a half after Columbus sailed to the westward. More than twice that number of years have since fallen slowly into history, like stones dropping down into the sea. From the outside, she must seem to be top-heavy with traditions; yet of them all, according to Morison, the only Harvard institutions truly deserving the title ancient are the Charter, the Corporation, the Honorable and Reverend the Board of Overseers, the names of the four undergraduate classes, and the ceremony of Commencement. Harvard did not become a university in the accepted sense till the embryonic Medical School was founded in 1782, some years after Columbia and Pennsylvania had begun giving instruction in medicine. Before the Revolution, the Corporation had served less as an administrative council than as a group of teaching fellows; and the last vestige of State control over College affairs was not eliminated till 1865, when certain officers of the Commonwealth who were *ex officio* Overseers were replaced by holders of the A.B. and A.M. degrees elected by the alumni. The term Faculty was substituted for The Immediate Government only in the 1820's. Written examinations, precursors of the finals, were not instituted till 1857; and the faculty continued to carry the heavy burden of daily classroom recitations for another thirty years, when also the three *cum laude* degrees were introduced. Courses were called studies before 1872, at about which time the College dropped its rules against smoking in the Yard and visiting the theater in Boston. Though Harvard was the first American college to abolish compulsory chapel—thus confirming her ancient reputation for godlessness—this revolutionary step was not actually taken until 1886, with the Old Guard opposed as usual. In compensation, however, class attendance was first taken in the same year; and in 1869 the old Scale of Merit system of marking—the "horrible system" introduced by Quincy, which sought to grade students on the scale of 8, with deductions for disciplinary infrac-

tions (not unlike the method still used at West Point and Annapolis)—gave way to the present system.

The pedigree of Harvard's notorious "indifference" is less certain. Morison rather engagingly attributes it to the mask of indifference cultivated by the undergraduates to hide their chagrin in winning only two Yale football games during the eighties and nineties. But George Birkbeck Hill, author of *Harvard College by an Oxonian* (1894), blames it on the rigid early-nineteenth-century system of instruction that discouraged original talent and engendered an attitude of *laissez faire* which gradually became the fashionable undergraduate pose, and quotes Dr. William Ellery Channing (A.B. 1798) to prove his point.

No, Harvard is older in years than in tradition except, undoubtedly, with regard to her ancient and still ardent devotion to the principle of freedom.

When my three little girls spent a winter's schooling in France, the youngest failed, to put it mildly, to distinguish herself academically. Yet when prize day came along and the awards were distributed she too received her little ribbon from the smiling schoolmistress—with an affectionate pat on the head to go with it—for *sagesse, bonne humeur, et philosophie*. Except in their wider sense these virtues do not and cannot count towards a college degree. General education in a free society must train men "to think effectively, to communicate thought, to make relevant judgments, to discriminate among values" and, while they're about it—let us hope—to live amicably with other free men. During the process the luckier student may even achieve the first faint bloom on the fruit of cultivation.

Four years are none too long: so many skins must be shed, so many new layers grown or grafted. If it be true that the first milestone on the road leading out of childhood is the discovery that your mother and father don't like spinach either, the next is perhaps the ability to tell an honest man from a scoundrel, and a third the precious lesson that because a thing is new, or because it is old, it is not therefore necessarily good: that the word "modern," fetish of youth and the advertising profession, is no more synonymous with "excellent" than the word "ancient." The knowledge that the integrity of the man who pushes the button is more important than the reliability of the machine the button starts is another item that hopeful but incredulous youth finds hard to accept, but must accept, if his education is to do him any good. The lesson of humility—hallmark of the truly great—can hardly be learned in four years;

but a beginning can be made, a glimpse caught. The downy freshman looks at a classmate a little timidly, a little truculently, thinking "I'm just as good as you are!" Four years later he may have learned to change the emphasis, saying "You're just as good as I am." Simple humility is not easily won. But it is a step on the road to becoming a free man and an educated man, and may at last enable one to apply to himself the aphorism "that man is free who is conscious of himself as the law which he obeys."

Who is wise enough to swear that the air he breathes, the sound of echoing footsteps of generations of great men who have gone before, the impalpable influences which shape and form the spirit as well as the mind, do not play their part in these beginnings?

Charles M. Flandrau's *The Diary of a Freshman* (1901)—that shining mirror of youth!—provides one answer to this question and, despite differences in educational emphasis, offers evidence that (except for changes wrought by the horseless carriage) neither youth nor Harvard has altered very much in the last fifty years:

The spring is scarcely over, and yet I've already begun to look forward to it again next year . . . In May and June bleak, shabby Cambridge covers all its angles and corners. They are softened and filled with billows and jets and sprays and garlands—green, gold, silver, mauve, and—what is the color of apple blossoms? They are such a tremor of white and pink that I never really know. The wind loses its bite, and then its chill. The air is moist and warm, and as you walk slowly through the quiet leafy streets at night, the damp, fresh lilac stretch out to dabble against your face, and something—it may be the stillness and sweetness of it all, or it may be just the penetrating smell of the box hedges—something makes you very sad and very happy at the same time . . . It was such a beautiful night that when we got to our gate, it seemed like wasting something to go in the house. Berri had finished his grind and was leaning out of my window. He said that his brain felt like a dead jellyfish (I think that was the pretty simile), and told us not to go in, as he would put on his coat and come down to us. So we strolled, all three, over to the Yard, and sat on the steps in front of one of the Holworthy entries. It was very late, but the finals were not yet over, and the yellow of many windows blurred through

the trees. The long quadrangle was flecked with moonlight, and little groups like our own were sitting in front of almost every doorway. The Yard that night seemed particularly quiet—a kind of lull before the crash of Class Day and Commencement. Duggie and Berri and I sat there talking until the air and the sky had changed from summer night to summer morning. Even then a few of the windows were still glowing.

Samuel Chamberlain's art turns physical Harvard into something New Englanders understand: the beauty not of formal design but of age. Taken separately, few of the College buildings measure up to an ideal aesthetic standard. ("One of the greatest benefits of a course at Harvard, Rollo," said Uncle George, as they descended the steps, "is that derived from viewing the noble architectural specimens which are all around you.") Yet each may be said to represent the best taste of the generation in which it was erected. Doubtless each was called badly designed, radical, daring, modern, mad, by contemporary embalmers. The Victorian Gothic of Memorial Hall, the Richardson Romanesque of Sever, the Coolidge Georgian of the Houses, each offers a good example of the best in "modern" taste, which goes not by fixed criteria but by fashion. Because of their warm cloak of age, Stoughton, Hollis, Holworthy, Harvard, Massachusetts, Holden Chapel, and Bulfinch's University Hall alone are beyond criticism—though from the number of internal operations performed on all of them, one is tempted to believe that respect for their age is only skin-deep. Architects may disagree about the College Church, but not the laymen, who find its clean and graceful lines appropriate and inspiring. Holworthy, severely functional, has the same beauty one discovers in the little red small-town mills which have been using the power of New England streams for almost as long as the old dormitories have been soothing the undergraduate breast. Each has the charm of good proportion and mellowing age. We like to look at them, and warm our sentimental hearts with the memory of the great dead who lived in them as young men. Only Widener, of the buildings in the Yard—and I do not except even Matthews, Weld, and Thayer—may justly be pronounced a total calamity, in function, in proportion and size, in all respects. The fault may be laid to an administration which was afraid to challenge the design for fear of losing the building: good New England doctrine, whatever else may be said of it. Though each building may be open to criticism, taken together they possess an inspiring harmony. New Englanders have always been "partial to a nice view," indeed our aesthetic sense may be said to begin and end with an appreciation of natural beauty. Distrust of "mere" physical beauty is supposedly inherent in the Puritan tradition, which preferred moral and spiritual grace. Eliot and Lowell, sound Unitarians both, were aesthetically almost purblind. Eliot made Harvard a great university: when he took office in 1869 he inherited a faculty of twenty-three, and five hundred and twenty-nine students. Seventeen years later the teaching staff had grown to sixty-one and the undergraduate body had more than doubled. One of his rare aesthetic opinions asserted that Romney should never have stooped to painting a hussy like Lady Hamilton. Yet he stood firmly behind Charles Eliot Norton's infant Fine Arts Department against strong faculty opposition. Similarly, in 1917, when the Harvard family exploded in an unrivaled display of angry fireworks over Archibald T. Davison's successful plot to turn the old bull-frog-on-the-bank Glee Club into a choral society, it was tone-deaf President Lowell who supported this devoted apostle of mature music to the limit of his great influence. Yet the same Lowell, who housed all Harvard, sincerely believed it more important to translate ten million Harkness dollars into bricks and mortar than to pause for an aesthetic ideal to take slow form. A Yankee administration could hardly do otherwise and remain true to itself and its tradition. Throughout Harvard history there have been similar compromises between the ideal and the practical, and not only in physical Harvard. The wonder is that the Yard remains as comely as it is. They who remember it before 1910, when the beetles killed the hundred-year-old elms, know how much those towering trees contributed, and how much their junior fellows are beginning to help today. Not in the laboratories but here in the Yard, Harvard shows her true face. It has the spiritual grace of a handsome old New England lady, the kind who likes to take up Greek or physics at eighty to keep her mind alert, scarcely aware of how beautifully her character shines through the marks and wrinkles, as she looks back with few regrets, gazes forward with calm courage.

Since the vanished elms were planted in 1815 and the original paths laid out from building to building, door to door, a crisscross of new walks have appeared in the Yard, beaten out by the students' footsteps. Here and there are fences, some high, some low. But the short cuts are not fenced: the muddy or dusty tracks appear, then one fine morning the impatient undergraduate finds that official notice has courteously been taken of his trespasses, in the form of fresh gravel. A new dormitory, chapel, or library is built, a new star discovered, a great teacher is born, science pushes the mysterious curtain back another millimetre: presto! the new pathways appear. Harvard is too experienced to call them royal roads, wise enough to know that time is the precious factor which alone may prove their worth.

Donald Moffat.

FAIR HARVARD

One of the original elms, planted in 1810, rises gracefully over Harvard's oldest surviving building, Massachusetts Hall (1720).

To the west, the spire of the First Church, Unitarian, of Cambridge soars above the chimneys and dormers of Massachusetts Hall.

Looking east, past Massachusetts, towards University Hall.

In its early days, Massachusetts contained thirty-two chambers, each with two smaller studies. At the west end were the College Bell and the College Clock, the face of which is painted much as it was over two centuries ago. Used as barracks for Continental troops during the siege of Boston in 1775, it was remodeled in 1821 to provide recitation rooms on the ground floor, and again in 1870 to include additional lecture rooms on the second floor. After the 1924 fire, it was restored to its original use as a dormitory, and shortly after President Conant's inauguration the executive offices were moved from University to the two lower floors. Here are shown two views of the Perkins Room, used by the Harvard Corporation for its monthly meetings. The President and Fellows of Harvard College is the oldest corporation in the United States existing under its original charter.

The Duplessis portrait of Franklin hangs over the fireplace in the President's office on the ground floor of Massachusetts Hall.

Mr. Conant's table was formerly used by both Mr. Eliot and Mr. Lowell. The cabinet (right) is dated 1681.

In 1916 the Lower Hall of Massachusetts was used by Professor George P. Baker for his famous course in playwriting, the "47 Workshop."

The Treaty of Utrecht, in 1713, inaugurated an era of peace, prosperity, and expansion in New England. In November, 1718, there were 124 students in residence; but Old Harvard and Stoughton College accommodated no more than 75. The Overseers, declaring in Biblical language that "the Numbers of the Sons of the Prophet are now so increas'd, that the Place where they were wont to dwell is become so Streight," petitioned the Massachusetts General Court for a new residential hall; and Massachusetts was erected at the public charge at a cost of £3500, leaving a balance of £116, which was presented to the Committee by the Court "in joyful surprise at their not exceeding the appropriation." Shown at the left is the east entry of Massachusetts Hall.

Above, Harvard Hall and a corner of Hollis. Right, the Johnston Gate. The site of this gate, facing west between Massachusetts and Harvard Halls, has been the main entrance to the Yard since the 17th century. In the bad old town-and-gown days, this area was an undergraduate rallying ground. In 1812 the students patriotically organized the Harvard Washington Corps, a swagger company that paraded in blue coats, white vests, trousers, and gaiters—to be elected Captain was one of the most coveted college honors. But the Corps was not much liked by the citizen soldiery, who on one occasion pursued the slender Washingtonians at point of bayonet to the Yard gate, when suddenly appeared the gray-haired Professor of Greek, Dr. Popkin, shouting, "Now my lads, stand your ground, you're in the right now! Don't let one of them set foot within the College grounds!" And so Mercury vanquished Mars.

Harvard Hall was built in 1766 on the site of Old Harvard, destroyed by fire in 1764 with the entire College library of 5000 volumes. It was the first college building that included no chambers and studies. The ground floor room on the east end was the College Hall. Even after commons were removed to University Hall in 1815, and until Memorial Hall was built in 1874, this hall remained *the* college hall, and was used for commencement dinners and class day dances. The room on the west end was the New Chapel, replacing Holden. The college kitchen in the east basement continued to be one of the sights of Cambridge. The new library and Philosophical Chamber (where Kittredge later conducted English 2) were situated upstairs. Above, Harvard and Massachusetts from University Hall. Below, the steps of Harvard.

The money for building Harvard Hall was provided by the Massachusetts General Court, whose members felt responsibility for the fire of 1764 by reason of their temporary occupation of Old Harvard, having been driven from Boston by the smallpox. Considering that 640 soldiers were quartered in Massachusetts in 1775, a like number in Hollis, 240 in Stoughton, and 160 in little Holden, it is surprising how little damage was done. Much of the interior woodwork and most of the brass doorknobs and locks on the studies disappeared, and half a ton of lead from the roof of Harvard was molded into bullets to speed the British from Boston. But the total loss was valued at less than £450, which the State assumed. The lower picture shows the west door of Holden Chapel, with Lionel on the right, and Harvard's rear elevation in the background.

Holden served as a chapel for only twenty years. In 1783 the Medical Department used it for a dissecting amphitheater, hence it has been called "the cradle of the Harvard Medical School."

Above, the back of Harvard Hall and a corner of Lionel Hall, one of the small dormitories built along the edge of the Yard in 1926. Right, Holden Chapel. Thomas Hutchinson, future royal governor, was responsible for obtaining from Mrs. Samuel Holden of London £400 to build a college chapel. Holden Chapel, a little gem of Georgian architecture designed in London, with Mrs. Holden's arms magnificently achieved on the east pediment, was completed in 1744. Besides serving as chapel and dissecting room, it has also been used at various times as a fire-engine house, lumber room, lecture hall, museum, and temporary home of the departments of Philosophy, Music, and Public Speaking.

Phillips Brooks House (1900), the college social-service center, and the back of Stoughton.

Emerson and Thoreau roomed in Hollis; and from 1904 to 1932, in Hollis 15, "Copey" kept open house on "Wednesday evenings after ten."

Stoughton (right), built from the proceeds of a state lottery, was placed according to Charles Bulfinch's original plan for the Old Yard.

The Old Yard, looking south from Holworthy (below). In 1768 we first hear of a "liberty tree" or "rebellion elm," opposite the middle of Hollis, where the students assembled to organize resistance against imaginary acts of oppression. The seniors threatened, if their "rights" were not respected, to go to Yale; but this desperate measure could not be carried out lacking a recommendation from President Holyoke.

Above, Stoughton, with Holworthy on the right—the west entry. The famous Rebellion of 1834 started with the freshmen and sophomores striking against Dr. Beck, the Latin professor, when he compelled them to memorize Zumpft's *Latin Grammar*—a mere look into which is enough to give one a headache. The faculty, as usual, attempted to "make an example" of a few students; their classmates protested, at first by petition, then by breaking the tutors' windows and ringing the college bell in the middle of the night. On May 29, all the sophomores were dismissed for the year by President Quincy, who announced that since those responsible for breaking the windows could not be discovered, the Grand Jury of Middlesex County would be invoked to root out the offenders and proceed against them by civil process. Then, hell broke loose! The "black flag of rebellion" was hung from the roof of Holworthy; a terrific explosion took place in chapel, and President Quincy was hanged in effigy from the Rebellion Tree.

Above, Thayer Hall from Hollis, in front of which a replica of one of the old Yard pumps now stands. In the 1850's "modern conveniences" began to make their timid appearance. Holworthy was lighted by gas from 1855, and other halls followed suit. Grays Hall, built in 1863, was the first college building to have water taps in the basement; other denizens of the Yard had to obtain their water from the Yard pumps, or hire one of the college porters—Big Mike, Little Mike, or Dirty Mike—to lug it in. Fastidious youths who wanted plumbing had to room in private houses. Below, the south portico of the Memorial Church seen between Thayer and University Halls.

It may be assumed that John Harvard rode over from Charlestown to Cambridge in the early summer of 1638, and was sufficiently impressed with what was going on to help the good work along. And although death came speedily, in death John did not forget the College. We have no details of his last illness; we only know that on September 14, 1638, John Harvard died at Charlestown of tuberculosis. By an oral will he left half his property and all his library to the College. As Thomas Shepard, a contemporary, wrote, "the man was a Scholler and pious in his life and enlarged toward the cuntry and the good of it in life and death." On the occasion of Harvard's 250th anniversary, Daniel Chester French was commissioned to execute this ideal statue of the young John Harvard. First placed in the Delta, it was later moved to its present position in front of University. At the same time a new heraldic seal was adopted for the College Arms, with *Veritas* restored to the three open books, whence it had been banished in 1848 by Everett during his brief and stormy presidency.

University Hall (1815) was designed by Bulfinch as the center of his plan for the Old Yard. Commons were located on the first floor and were divided into four rooms, one for each class, with circular apertures between, which offered tempting openings through which insults and bread could could be hurled from one class to another. On the second and third floors were recitation rooms and the President's office.

President Kirkland (1810-28) found the Yard an "unkempt sheep-commons," almost treeless, with no regular paths, and cluttered with a brewhouse, the college woodyard, and a pigpen, where the Corporation's own porkers fought with rats for the commons garbage; for years the hideous clamor of a pig-killing was wont to disturb recitations in University. Under Kirkland, the famous elms were planted, paths laid out, and the mangy turf teased into becoming a proper lawn. Above, the west front of University; below, the east façade in winter.

The Faculty Room in University has seen many changes. Designed originally to serve as the College Chapel, (succeeding the old chapel in the west end of Harvard) and rising two stories in the middle of the building, it passed its churchly function on to Appleton Chapel when the latter was dedicated in 1858, and ten years later was cut in two horizontally, the upper half being used for examination rooms. In 1890 President Eliot combined the College and Scientific School Faculties to form the Faculty of Arts and Sciences, sixty-two strong. By 1896, the Faculty had so increased that larger quarters were needed to accommodate its meetings and the old chapel in University was restored to its present form, though without the original galleries. The old Bulfinch wainscoting and cornices were found intact, and new pilasters were added to match the old. Today this room, 55 x 45 x 30 feet high, and embellished with portraits and busts of presidents, professors, and benefactors, is one of Harvard's most distinguished rooms.

Matthews (above) and Weld Halls, facing each other across the southern end of the Yard, were built in 1872 from unsolicited funds given by two non-Harvard merchants of Boston, and Matthews promptly became known as "the finest dormitory in America." At this time there was an epidemic of bonfires in the Yard, started with heaps of lumber lying about; and each was the signal for the proctors and "Yard cops" to try to put them out. Professor Lanman's trundling off an old buggy filled with burning hay was a long-remembered event; and Eliot was once seen pulling a mattress off the flames, with a student at the other end trying to get it back. Finally the President had a bright idea. He ordered the proctors to keep to their rooms in the event of a bonfire; and the students, deprived of the delicious spectacle of distracted proctors, soon lost interest in that form of riot.

The south portico of the Memorial Church and, beneath the trees, the site of the Tercentenary Theater.

On Armistice Day, 1932, the Memorial Church was dedicated in the words inscribed under the south portico (above): *In grateful memory of the Harvard men who died in the World War we have built this Church.* Of modified colonial design, its traditional severity is softened by touches of color, especially in the south and west porticos with their Doric columns and wide steps. Above the south portico rises the tower, 172 feet to the top of the wooden spire and 197 feet to the tip of the weather vane. The bell, an anonymous gift to the University, was cast in Loughborough, England, and bears the inscription *In Memory of Voices that are Hushed.* Below, the Memorial Church from the north, with the Gate of the Classes of 1887 and 1888 at the right.

Above, the south portico of the Memorial Church, with a corner of Thayer Hall; and below, the west portico or main entrance. Inside the south portico, under the tower, is the Memorial Room, in which are inscribed the names of 373 Harvard men who died in World War I. The dedicatory inscription, which extends round the room in a frieze, was composed by President Lowell: "While a bright future beckoned, they freely gave their lives and fondest hopes for us and our allies, that we might learn from them courage in peace to spend our lives making a better world for others." Inside the Church itself, on the south wall, hangs the Service Flag of the University, representing 11,398 men who served in the United States and allied armed forces in that war.

The Sacrifice, a fallen knight with a sorrowing figure at his head, is a memorial to Robert Bacon, '80, United States Ambassador to France, and other Harvard men who died in World War I.

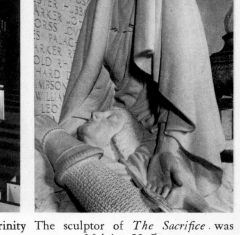

The pulpit, of English bog oak, was given by the vestry of **Trinity** Church, Boston, in memory of Phillips Brooks (A.B. 1855).

The sculptor of The Sacrifice was Malvina Hoffman.

The high white pews with mahogany rails, the gray and white walls and vaulted ceiling, are in the colonial tradition of church architecture. Below, a carved oak screen with gilt iron grille separates the main part of the Church from the choir, which retains the name of Appleton Chapel, built on the same site in 1858. It is paneled in oak throughout, with its pews arranged as stalls for the College Choir. The organ, divided between the two sides of the choir, was given in memory of Albert Keep Isham, '15. On the top of the case on the north side is carved the Isham family coat of arms.

Designed in 1880 by Henry H. Richardson, '49, Sever Hall is a perfect example of this architect's modern adaptation of the Romanesque. Used for recitations and lectures, its classrooms formerly boasted an unusually fine collection of carved wooden benches, the work of dreamy undergraduate penknife sculptors. Some of the newer generation of artists may be seen above, between classes. Below, the back of Sever, and (left) Emerson Hall, since its erection in 1905 the home of the Department of Philosophy.

Robinson Hall (above) was designed, when it was built in 1901, to house the Graduate School of Architecture. In 1936 Architecture, Regional Planning, and Landscape Architecture joined departmental forces, and Robinson has since been the home of the Graduate School of Design so formed. Sever Quadrangle (left), enclosed by Robinson, Sever, Emerson, and the Class of 1885 Gate and fence, tented over and filled with folding chairs and unfolding *puellae pulcherimae,* was the scene of many a Harvard Commencement on fair June days. Lately, since the latter years of the war, Commencements have been held in the larger Tercentenary Theater in the middle Yard.

The President's House (1912) stands on the site of an earlier presidential residence occupied successively by Felton, Hill, and Eliot.

Site of the Tercentenary Theater, 1936. The brilliantly gowned academic procession moved in the September rain from Widener Library (above) to a canopied dais along the south side of Memorial Church.

Widener's Farnsworth Room was designed for undergraduate pleasure reading in an atmosphere approximating that of a home library.

Widener's broad granite steps form the traditional concert platform for the Harvard Glee Club on pleasant May evenings.

Sever (left) and Emerson from the steps of Widener.

Two of Houghton Library's treasure rooms. Harvard's first library, housed in the "Old College," which stood near the present site of Grays Hall, was thought by some contemporaries "to be too gorgeous for a Wilderness." When its successor, Old Harvard, was burned to the ground in 1764, the entire library perished with it, but was promptly replaced by friends of the College and by a grant from the Province of New Hampshire. By 1816 the library had grown large enough to fill all of "new" Harvard's second floor; and by 1829, "still thus wretchedly housed," it was considered the largest and most valuable collection of books and maps in North America. When Gore Hall was built—in 1841, of Quincy granite, in the Gothic style—the library had grown to 41,000 volumes. Though Gore was planned to meet the needs of the College for seventy-five years, it was already filled by 1863, when new floors and wings were grafted on, and was torn down in 1912 to make way for Widener. By then the library had swelled to half a million books, which have since overflowed into Houghton, and into the neighboring Lamont Library, begun in 1947 from a bequest of the late Thomas W. Lamont, '92, one of Harvard's great benefactors.

This stone dragon and tablet, a Tercentenary gift of the Harvard Club of China, stands on the lawn at the west side of Widener.

Between Boylston Hall (right), Harvard's first science building, and two Wigglesworth dormitories (left), is a distant view of Wadsworth House.

Wadsworth House (1727), the second oldest Harvard building now standing, was built and named for Harvard's tenth president, and in 1775 served as General Washington's headquarters. After Wadsworth, nine successive presidents lived in it, Edward Everett (1846-9) being the last. Miss Maria, one of President Quincy's four unmarried daughters, thus describes a gala Commencement of 1829 in her journal: "The family were up early to roll the diplomas and tie them with blue ribbons. At nine the girls joined the press around the doors of the meeting-house; and when these were opened, what a scramble! Ladies running, and screaming as they ran; ladies vaulting over the backs of pews to secure good seats . . . At five-thirty, gentlemen and ladies began to pour into Wadsworth House; ladies in drawing-room, band in back parlor; Governor and aides and distinguished foreigners arriving and departing till half past seven, ice-creams and coffee circulating all the time." The front door (right) gave upon a pleasant garden until Massachusetts Avenue was widened.

Wadsworth's two wings were added to the original structure in 1783; the brick ell (moved in 1871 to adjoin it) was built in 1810.

The picturesque office of the Secretary of the Harvard Alumni Association is on the ground floor of Wadsworth House.

Grays (left), Wadsworth House, and (right) a corner of Lehman, looking south towards the Class of 1857 Gate and Massachusetts Avenue.

These ancient beeches shade the small triangular plot between Wadsworth House and Lehman Hall. This may have been the site of the stable in which President Wadsworth kept his horse "until it reached the mature age of twenty-three, when he turned it in with £25 to boot for a dull and waspish eight-year-old." The old Bradish meadow across the street (the site of Holyoke House) was a presidential perquisite, and one of the unpaid duties of freshmen was to make the President's hay. Massachusetts Avenue was a mere lane in the 18th century, called "the way to the Parsonage," then situated about opposite Plympton Street at the edge of the present Yard. The Charlestown Road (Kirkland Street) and Wood (Boylston) Street were the main roads from Boston into Cambridge. Left, the spire of the First Church, Unitarian, rises above the roof of Straus Hall, one of the small dormitories built in 1926 to cloister the Yard, with the front elevation of Lehman Hall seen at the left.

Lehman Hall (1924) houses the University's business offices. In the 17th century there were two financial officers, the Treasurer, who made investments, collected rents, and paid salaries, and the Steward, who acted as bursar, purchasing agent, superintendent of buildings, and caterer. The records of the Steward's office go back to 1650, when many poor students met their term bills with payments of grain, cattle, and garden produce. "The expense of a college life at Cambridge is very great . . . near $300 a year," wrote a freshman in 1816 — and no wonder, with the tuition raised from $20 a year in 1817 to $55 in 1825. Lehman Hall stands on the site of Dane Hall, which burned in 1918, first home of the Harvard Law School. The main entrance of Lehman (right) faces east towards the Yard. The doorway is considered a particularly fine adaptation of early Georgian architecture.

The Class of 1875 Gate leads into the Yard from Harvard Square, between Lehman and Straus. Across the Square, the "Harvard Coop."

Looking westward along Massachusetts Avenue past the McKean Gate, towards Harvard Square. As late as 1856 there were only a dozen shops around the Square, which was shaded by a great elm. But every year more brick blocks with shops on the ground floor replaced the wooden dwellings. Old Cambridge "grows a little more citylike every day," wrote Charles Eliot Norton to his cousin Charles W. Eliot in 1864. "I confess I do not like this process of suburbanization — or the results of it. The old town was better in the days when we were boys, my dear Charles!" And "the passage of the horse-cars to and from Boston nearly, if not quite, a hundred times a day, has rendered it practically impossible for the Government of the College to prevent our young men from being exposed to the temptations of the city," declared President Hill in his report for 1863. Right, the Class of 1877 Gate enters the Yard directly behind Widener. Beyond, a corner of Wigglesworth, named after a Massachusetts family whose first Harvard representative was Michael Wigglesworth (A.B. 1651).

At the Meyer Gate we leave the Yard for the North Country, where labor men of Law and Science.

Looking east across the Old Burying Ground towards
the Yard, with the First Church, Unitarian, on the
right, and the spire of the Memorial Church, the cupola
of Harvard Hall, and Memorial Hall tower seen
through bare winter branches. Right, Christ Church,
facing the Common just west of the Burying Ground.
The old wooden church is a fine specimen of the
austerely gracious colonial Georgian style of church
architecture. Established in 1759 as a mission for the
Society for the Propagation of the Gospel in Foreign
Parts, it ministered to Church of England families in
Cambridge and to students of Harvard College. At the
time of the Revolution most of the Tory congregation
followed the British Army to Nova Scotia.

Memorial Hall (1878) from the west or Delta end, as it looked before the tower decorations were removed. for safety's sake, in 1945.

Sanders Theater and Memorial Hall from the east. The Sanders Theater concerts of the Boston Symphony Orchestra were begun in 1881.

Littauer Center, home of the Graduate School of Public Administation, was erected in 1938, on the site of the old Hemenway Gymnasium, from funds given the University by Lucius N. Littauer, '78. Here promising graduate students, including many officials on leave from the government service, explore the problems of city, state, and nation, and undertake research in the social sciences over a broad range of questions relating to public policy and administration. The Faculty is drawn from the University, principally from the departments of Government and Political Economy.

Looking west towards (left to right) the back of Littauer, Gannett House, the new Hemenway Gymnasium, and the Law School's Austin Hall.

Once used as a dormitory, Gannett House (*c.* 1830) now contains the offices of the Harvard Law Review and other Law School activities.

The visit of Prince Henry of Prussia in 1902 brought to a culmination Professor Hugo Francke's efforts to establish a Germanic Museum; the first collection, in the Old Gymnasium, was opened in 1903. Above, the Germanic Museum today. It was built in 1917 from funds donated by Adolphus Busch, and is particularly noted for its outstanding collection of medieval sculpture in reproduction. Left, Austin Hall (1883) contains four large Law School lecture rooms, a reading room, and part of the Law Library. It was designed in the Romanesque style by Henry H Richardson, architect of Sever Hall.

The Germanic Museum.

The Music Building (1914). Music was the only subject added to the curriculum during the regime of stone-deaf President Walker (1853-60).

Langdell Hall (1907). In 1870, Eliot appointed as Professor of Law young Christopher Columbus Langdell, father of the famous case system and Dean of the great faculty including Holmes, Gray, Thayer, and Ames.

Mallinckrodt Laboratory (1928). Until Boylston Hall was built in 1858, the first chemical laboratory was in the basement of University Hall.

Home of the mathematical "brain," Harvard's famous Computation Laboratory.

The Anechoic Chamber. Here are explored the properties of sound sources and sound receivers, unmodified by echoes, hence anechoic.

Above, a rhododendron, one of the Ware Collection of Glass Flowers, since the 1890's probably Harvard's most renowned possession. The work of two Bohemian naturalists, Leopold Blaschka and his son Rudolph, these exquisite reproductions of 164 plant families are the product of no secret method, but of pure technical skill and artistry on the part of two men of matchless scientific integrity and devotion. The University Museum, child of the great Louis Agassiz, was begun in 1859 and finished in 1915 after the death of Alexander Agassiz, who had succeeded his father as director in 1874. Louis Agassiz raised the money, persuaded the University to grant the land, and gathered round him a corps of young naturalists destined to great careers—Lyman, Hyatt, Putnam, Shaler, and Verill among them. The Museum, a large U-shaped building, consists of the Museum of Comparative Zoology, the Botanical Museum, the Geological and Mineralogical Museums, and (left) the Peabody Museum of American Archaeology and Ethnology.

The Biological Laboratories, devoted to the study of living organisms. The bas-reliefs and animal sculptures are the work of Katharine Lane.

The Divinity School's Andover Hall (1911). It was in 1838, when old Divinity Hall was twelve years old that young Emerson delivered his *Divinity School Address*, a landmark in American thought.

Two interesting versions of Gothic
Revival architecture. Farlow House
(above), now headquarters of the
Graduate School of Arts and Sciences, is a good example on the
domestic scale. Memorial Hall, with
its massive contours, here seen from
the corner of Divinity Avenue and
Kirkland Street, is superbly unique;
even if changing tastes have made
it unappetizing to many present-day
palates, it cannot be ignored.

The main entrance of the Fogg Art Museum (1927) on Quincy Street. Its predecessor, in the Yard facing Broadway, has been renamed Hunt Hall.

The Fogg Art Museum, two interior views. President Eliot inherited little aesthetic sense from his ancestors and had acquired less from his education, but he was distinctly not a Philistine; and when Norton urged him to find a place in Harvard for the Fine Arts, he responded. The Department opened in 1874, and Norton's famous lectures for twenty-four years were the principal means of inculcation in our "young barbarians at play" an urbane and civilized point of view. His successors—Post, Pope, Porter, Sachs, Forbes—have carried on and enlarged upon Norton's principles. As expressed by one of the Directors, "the purpose of a university Fine Arts Department is not the creation of artists. It is to give a large number of men a familiarity with the art heritage of our civilization, and to a limited number the training and experience necessary to enable them to serve as curators and directors of museums, or connoisseurs, critics, and teachers of the arts."

The old yellow Dana-Palmer house was moved in 1947 to its present site between the Faculty Club (left) and the Harvard Union (above, right) to make way for the new Lamont Library at the corner of Massachusetts Avenue and Quincy Street. Dating from 1820, and for ten years thereafter the home of Richard Henry Dana, it became in 1840 the first Harvard Astronomical Observatory, with a revolving turret installed on the roof. The beloved teacher of philosophy, George Herbert Palmer, lived in it from 1894 until his death in 1933. The stone post-and-rail fence along the east side of this part of Quincy Street, typical of a lost simplicity, is one of the few surviving bits of fence that once enclosed various parts of the Yard.

Passing south from the Yard, we look down Plympton Street towards the river, with (right) Randolph Hall, now an Adams House dormitory, and (left) the gold cupola of the main building of Adams House.

Above, Apthorp House (1760), residence of the Master of Adams House, and (left) Lampy's hard hat and ivy-bearded visage, with Randolph Hall, former Gold Coast dormitory, on Bow Street beyond. Apthorp House, hidden from the street, is a Georgian dwelling of charm and dignified proportions. In the winter of 1777-8, to accommodate Burgoyne's surrendered army, General Heath, who had to find quarters somewhere for the prisoners, made every effort to procure the college buildings, and the students were sent home in late November; but the Corporation got its back up and refused to hand over anything but a wooden dwelling to the Army. In the end, barracks were found for the British troops; "Gentleman Jack" Burgoyne and his staff occupied Apthorp House, so the net result was three months' winter vacation for the students. Most of the area between what is now Mt. Auburn Street and the river was swampy land, inundated by the tidal Charles, until it was gradually reclaimed and, eventually, acquired by the University through the efforts of a few devoted and far-sighted friends.

The Signet Society, founded in 1870, is a literary and social club whose membership is primarily devoted to the liberal arts.

Randolph Hall, the Lampoon Building, the tower of St. Paul's Catholic Church, and the Fly Club.

The east façade and steps of the Indoor Athletic Building, built in 1930, the gift of three anonymous donors

Kirkland House is composed of Smith Halls (left) and Bryan Hall, former freshman dormitories. In the background, the Master's Lodgings.

The courtyard of Kirkland House, named for Rev. John Thornton Kirkland, president from 1810 to 1828, the "Augustan Age of Harvard."

Above, Hicks House (1762). On April 20, 1775, Percy's column covered the disastrous British retreat from Lexington, fighting minutemen most of the way; in a skirmish near Porter's Station were killed Major Isaac Gardner of Brookline, first Harvard man to fall in the Revolutionary War, and John Hicks of Cambridge, whose ancient dwelling is now the library of Kirkland House. Left, Smith Hall from Boylston Street.

The courtyard of Kirkland House in winter.

A corner of Bryan Hall, with the adjoining Master's Lodgings beyond.

Doorway to the Master's Lodgings, Kirkland House.

During the administration of President Eliot (1869-1909), for whom Eliot House (above) is named, Harvard College was transformed into a university.

Eliot House from the north end of the Weeks Bridge, with the Anderson Bridge, leading to Soldiers Field, and the Weld Boathouse (1907).

Eliot House and the site of the old college wharf, where the wood-sloops once discharged their cargoes of Maine firewood.

The southwest corner of Eliot House faces the football crowds returning from Soldiers Field across the Anderson Bridge.

Above, Eliot House, with Dunster House in the distance. The gateway (above and left) leads into the Great Court of Eliot House. The meeting rooms of the Society of Fellows, graduate students chosen from all parts of the country for their promise of notable contribution to knowledge, look out upon the Master's Court.

A corner of the Master's Lodgings, Eliot House, and the court.

One of the gates to the hexagonal Great Court of Eliot House.

The traditional Eliot House play, an Elizabethan drama, is given each year before Christmas.

In 1878 the boathouses acquired floats—no longer at low tide did crews have to lower their shells into the water and slide down the piles like fishermen—but the floats were still flanked by coal and wood wharves.

An arched doorway leads into one of the inner courts of the Graduate School of Business Administration, situated south of the river.

The Business School Faculty Club, with Eliot House over the river.

Hamilton, Sherman, and Morris Halls, Business School dormitories, looking east.

Right, the Business School's Baker Library is named for George F. Baker, who gave the buildings and endowed the school "to promote knowledge and integrity in the art of finance, industry, and commerce."

This Soldiers Field shaft was erected by Major Henry Lee Higginson to commemorate friends who fell in the Civil War. Beyond, Briggs Cage and Dillon Field House.

Dillon Field House, given by Clarence Dillon, '05, provides locker and dressing rooms for all varieties of Soldiers Field athletics.

John Winthrop House comprises former freshman dormitories Gore (above) and Standish Halls. Named for the Governor of Massachusetts Bay Colony who became the Harvard Board of Overseers' first chairman.

Standish Hall, of John Winthrop House, looks upon the river. Beyond, the graceful tower of Lowell House

The north face of Standish Hall. On the right of the entry is the Winthrop House Library, on the left the Senior Common Room.

Winthrop House through an arch of the Anderson Bridge.

The Master's Lodgings, Lowell House.

Lowell House. Above, the Master's residence and (right) the Dining Hall. One day in the fall of 1928, Edward S. Harkness (Yale '97), walked into Mr. Lowell's office and offered him three million dollars to build and endow an "honor College." It took Mr. Lowell about ten seconds to accept. The Governing Boards took up the plan with such alacrity that Mr. Harkness soon increased his offer to ten millions for equipping no less than seven houses for the three upper classes. Thus a Yale man became the greatest benefactor in Harvard history, making a noble return for the part that Harvard men had taken in founding his alma mater.

In Lowell House tower hangs a Russian *zvon*, or chime of seventeen bells, the gift of Charles R. Crane.

The terraced courts of Lowell House impart a sense of cloistered intimacy to this, the most centrally located of the Houses.

In Lowell House Dining Hall hang portraits of distinguished members of the Lowell family.

On the north terrace of this court stands Daniel C. French's bust of James Russell Lowell, formerly located in the Yard.

An arched doorway leads into Lowell House courtyard

Beyond, the Indoor Athletic Building.

John Winthrop House, with the tower of Lowell House beyond, and the Weeks Memorial Bridge.

The river parkways were laid out after the building of the Charles River dam in 1910. Above, the towers of Eliot and Lowell.

Above and right, McKinlock Hall which, with Mather, forms Leverett House. Today, it is hard to believe that the "House Plan" was once as vigorously opposed as every other Harvard innovation. Seriously considered in 1871 and again in 1894, the plan was given up largely because President Eliot was too busy increasing Harvard's intellectual opportunities to care for the social side of college life. Even in 1928 the plan aroused stormy opposition: the Faculty objected to the way it was "railroaded through"; the *Crimson* denounced it; the students on the whole were hostile, preferring the traditional Harvard liberty to sink or swim alone, and dreading the specter of "boarding-school discipline."

Spring activity at the Weld Boathouse. To the right, the Weeks Memorial Bridge (1927) and the tower of Dunster House.

One of the fine doorways of Leverett House.

Dunster House was named for Henry Dunster, Harvard's first president.

Dunster House tower was inspired by the famous Big Tom tower of Christ Church, Oxford.

Above, Dunster House through an arch of the Weeks Bridge. On the central pediment under the tower, facing south, are the arms of Harvard University; on the west pediment appear those of Magdalen College, Cambridge, from which Henry Dunster graduated in 1631, and on the east pediment, the Dunster family arms. The isolation of Dunster House has nourished there a certain corporate spirit which, its students like to feel, retains a good deal of the easy individualism of an earlier Harvard. Left, the central court from the river side.

The central court gate was given in memory of Charles Chauncy Stillman (A.B. 1898), by his son, and bears the Stillman family arms.

The towers of Cambridge, left to right: Lowell House, the Memorial Church, Adams House, Memorial Hall, St. Paul's, and Dunster House.

Dunster House from the south bank of the frozen Charles.

Above and right, McKinlock Hall which, with Mather, forms Leverett House. Today, it is hard to believe that the "House Plan" was once as vigorously opposed as every other Harvard innovation. Seriously considered in 1871 and again in 1894, the plan was given up largely because President Eliot was too busy increasing Harvard's intellectual opportunities to care for the social side of college life. Even in 1928 the plan aroused stormy opposition: the Faculty objected to the way it was "railroaded through"; the *Crimson* denounced it; the students on the whole were hostile, preferring the traditional Harvard liberty to sink or swim alone, and dreading the specter of "boarding-school discipline."

Spring activity at the Weld Boathouse. To the right, the Weeks Memorial Bridge (1927) and the tower of Dunster House.

One of the fine doorways of Leverett House.

Dunster House was named for Henry Dunster, Harvard's first president.

Dunster House tower was inspired by the famous Big Tom tower of Christ Church, Oxford.

Above, Dunster House through an arch of the Weeks Bridge. On the central pediment under the tower, facing south, are the arms of Harvard University; on the west pediment appear those of Magdalen College, Cambridge, from which Henry Dunster graduated in 1631, and on the east pediment, the Dunster family arms. The isolation of Dunster House has nourished there a certain corporate spirit which, its students like to feel, retains a good deal of the easy individualism of an earlier Harvard. Left, the central court from the river side.

The central court gate was given in memory of Charles Chauncy Stillman (A.B. 1898), by his son, and bears the Stillman family arms.

The towers of Cambridge, left to right: Lowell House, the Memorial Church, Adams House, Memorial Hall, St. Paul's, and Dunster House.

Dunster House from the south bank of the frozen Charles.